IMAGES OF WALES

ROGERSTONE

IMAGES OF WALES

ROGERSTONE

KIM FRY

TEMPUS

Frontispiece: A general view of Rogerstone from the early 1900s showing upper Tregwilym Road. The large white building mid-left is the Tydu Hotel. On the extreme right the Castle Mound and the Mansion House are just visible.

First published 2005

Tempus Publishing Limited
The Mill, Brimscombe Port,
Stroud, Gloucestershire, GL5 2QG
www.tempus-publishing.com

British Library Cataloguing in Publication Data.
A catalogue record for this book is available from the British Library.

ISBN 0 7524 3506 X

Typesetting and origination by Tempus Publishing Limited.
Printed in Great Britain.

Contents

Members of the newly formed Rogerstone Local History Society. From left to right: Brian Stephen, Vernon Morgan, Kim Fry, Cliff Roberts and Derek Picken.

Acknowledgements

I would like to thank the following individuals whose kind donations of photographs and information made this book possible.

Nancy Appleby, Anthony Arscott, Mary Bailey, Edna Brown, Mrs M.E. Dee, Terry Dudley, Mrs V.M. Edwards, Charles Evans, the late Mr Jim Everson, Mary Fry, Beryl James, Alex Jarvis, A. Johnson, D. Jones, R. Jones, Malcolm Langley, Mr Lloyd, Roger Morgan, Vernon Morgan, Sylvia Northam, the late Eric Osment, Mike Phillips, Derek Picken, D. Picken (Canada) R. Robson, Mr Rosser, Keith Russell, Brian J. Stephen, Brian J.J. Stephen, Mrs M. Stephen, Brian Sullivan, Terry Watkins.

Also many thanks to the following for allowing use of maps, articles and photographs: Alcan, Rogerstone, Newport Museum & Art Gallery, Newport Reference Library, Ordnance Survey Office, D.R. Sach, Risca Industrial History Museum, *South Wales Argus*.

Introduction

I started off with an idea to create a 'timeline' with an exhibition of old photographs to celebrate the Rogerstone Library's centenary in 2005. This idea grew into a book after I had been repeatedly asked why the library did not have a book on the local history of Rogerstone. My work in the Newport Reference Library had shown me that there was indeed information about Rogerstone, but not in one source. Much of it was scattered paragraphs or pages within the history of the Parish of Bassaleg. As I began to gather this information together, so my Rogerstone Project was born.

The lack of photographs held by the library was my first stumbling block, but having heard of my project, a group of gentlemen also researching Rogerstone's local history invited me to attend one of their meetings. I was delighted to find that they had acquired a large collection of photographs and were very happy to assist me in this part of the project. Further donations of photographs began to arrive and I became optimistic that there would be a sufficient number to enable me to approach a publisher with a view to releasing a book to celebrate the library's centenary after all.

I hope the resultant book will provide the reader with as much pleasure as it gave me putting it together. The photographs show how a small village, situated near an old castle mound, grew into a large city suburb. But it also shows how, held together by the spirit of community during the hardships of two world wars and the Depression, it emerged as a growing, thriving community of the twenty-first century.

My sincerest thanks to Vernon Morgan, Derek Picken, Cliff Roberts and Brian Stephen for allowing me to become part of their group and without whose contributions this book would not have been possible.

A big Thank You to my friend and colleague Alex Jarvis for her enthusiasm, encouragement and help, and to Anne Edwards for assistance in 'digging up' information.

Kim Fry

In late 2003 I discovered some old Rogerstone and Bassaleg school photographs, which had been in my attic for years, mainly from 1938-47.

I took these along to the Whiteheads Sports Club to show friends who appeared in some of them. One most interested was Brian Stephen who suggested the possibility of arranging an evening to display our collections. At the same time Brian was attending the Redwood Club and realized that Derek Picken was also assembling a book of photographs of old Rogerstone as part of a family history project. A group was formed with Vernon Morgan who was known to have a lot of old photographs of Rogerstone. Soon afterwards it was also discovered that Kim of the Rogerstone Library was working on a project to commemorate the library's centenary. Kim was then invited to join the group, and thus the Rogerstone Local History Society was formed in September 2004.

I appreciate the honour of being its first chairman and give sincere thanks to the team and those who are supporting us in our venture of producing this book

Cliff Roberts

Rogerstone covers an area from the M4 motorway to the Welsh Oak public house near Pontymister in the lower part of the Ebbw Valley. It was, and sometimes still is, referred to as 'Top Rogy' and 'Bottom Rogy', especially by residents who have spent all their lives in the area. It was, of course, originally two hamlets, the top one being Tydu and the bottom one Tregwilym in an otherwise green field location. The name Rogy was known, not only locally, but over much of the Great Western Railway area as the little place in Wales from whence came many coal trains which kept industry going and houses warm. These assembled in a marshalling yard of vast proportions – in fact one of the largest on the GWR system – and this became the second largest employer in the village. The largest was the local steelworks of Guest Keen and Nettlefolds, which was eventually succeeded by aluminium works which remain to this day. Since the demise of the railway yard numerous light industries have been established to ensure employment for the residents.

We have a single track railway but no trains, as passenger services ended in around 1962 and freight trains finished very recently. It seems that, with the help of the National Assembly we may soon have our trains back hopefully to ease our road traffic problems. Buses we have in plenty, as they travel from the valleys through Rogerstone to both Newport and Cardiff.

We have always been known for a variety of sporting activities. Soccer came to Wales, and Rogerstone in particular, with the steelworkers from the Midlands, and cricket was fostered when an influx of railway men arrived from the West of England in the early twentieth century. We have had, and still have, choirs, bands, operatic societies etc. but the residents look more and more to the large cities for their entertainment.

There will always be a community spirit in our village and this came to the surface in times of disaster such as the Second World War when Rogerstone was hard hit by enemy activity. Unfortunately, some of our community activities, such as carnivals and Whit Monday walks of the churches, have had to be abandoned due to traffic problems. Church life, we are told, is in decline nationally, but in Rogerstone there are still seven active churches of the recognized denominations.

Thanks are due to the many people who have loaned photographs and other material to make this book possible. It is hoped that the resulting publication will be of interest to old and new residents alike.

Guidance from the publishers has been invaluable, particularly as this is the first time that a pictorial record of the area has been attempted on this scale. It has been achieved only as a result of the enthusiasm and dedication of Kim Fry supported by the officers of the recently formed Rogerstone Local History Society; Cliff Roberts, Brian Stephen, Derek Picken and Vernon Morgan.

Vernon Morgan

Rogerstone from Norman Times

The 'castle' site from which the village of Rogerstone has grown began its history in Norman times. After a battle near the Heath, Cardiff, in which the Welsh Lord of Glamorgan was slain, the Lordship of Wentlooge fell to Sir Roger Fitzhamon, who in turn divided up the lands under twelve 'marcher Lords'. One of these lords was Sir Robert de Haia, who governed the Bassaleg manor. As it was the custom for Normans to build an occupying castle upon lands granted to them, so Sir Robert chose 'the mound in the wide tideway, not far from Bassaleg church' for the site of his castle. Sir Robert's son Roger was the builder of this castle, probably between AD 1110 and 1120. The castle passed into the de Berkerolles family with the marriage of Roger de Haia's daughter Cecilia to Roger de Berkerolle, son of William, another of Fitzhamon's knights. There was also a tract of land included with the castle, the ground roughly covered nowadays from the castle site up to the Vicarage Corner, along the Cefn to High Cross, down to Pye Corner and back along to the Castle. William de Berkerolle governed this area and this is where the name Tre Gwilym originates. It is thought that the name Rogerstone came from Roger de Haia who built the castle. The castle then passed, through marriage, into the Stradling family who were forced to sell it to the Kemeys of Cefn Mably to raise money to pay the ransom for the release of Sir Thomas Stradling who was captured by pirates. By 1645, according to the diary of Richard Symonds, who accompanied King Charles I, the castle had disappeared, there no longer being a need for it. In 1700 Edward Morgan of Penllwyn Sarph and Bedwellty held the manor of Rogerstone, it eventually coming into the Herbert family.

The Castle Mansion House

The Rogerstone Castle Mansion was reputed to have been built on the castle mound site in the seventeenth century. There would have been glorious views of the River Ebbw and the valley below and possibly the church tower in Bassaleg. The building consisted of a basement, which incorporated the pantry, kitchen, scullery, cellar stores and a tunnel that might possibly have been part of Rogerstone Castle's service buildings. The first floor comprised 'entrance hall, parlour and bay windowed dining room', the second floor of three bedrooms, and the attic provided additional accommodation, probably servants' quarters. Part of the wall structure was said to be in places seven feet thick, one such wall on the works side rising from deep in the ground at an angle until reaching up to form part of the house wall. The rear wall was of equal thickness and through this the basement was to be found. The stone wall on the road side corner of the Mansion House continued back to where it joined with the reputed original castle out-buildings, quite a distance away, and probably the result of 'tidying up' of the old stable buildings: Upon arrival of Nettlefolds Ltd staff in 1885, the Mansion House was used as the Works Offices, until the stone-built Main Offices were completed in 1887. The red brick extension to those offices was added in 1900 thus making provision for the increased staff owing to the Works expansions and greatly increased productions. After the vacation of the Castle Mansion for the new offices, company officials continuously tenanted the mansion. The managing director of the works continued to lunch there until the 1930s. By 1938 the house had greatly deteriorated and was eventually demolished in 1986.

Kim Fry

The information and quotes in the Castle Mansion House paragraph are from an undated document on Rogerstone Castle (held by Newport Reference Library) by an unknown author.

Castle Mansion House showing the bay windowed dining room.

The rear of the house shows its much run-down state. These photographs were taken in 1978.

one

Industry

Early Industry

Early references to works on or near the castle site are made by John Bedford of Worcestershire, who refers to the building of a new forge at 'Rocheston' in October 1766. Snell's map of Monmouthshire dated 1785 shows copper mills in this area, and tin mills are marked on a number of maps dated in the early 1800s. Coxe writes of Rogerstone Castle in 1800 and mentions 'adjoining works on the bank of the Ebbw belonging to the Royal Mine Company', but the castle remains do not appear to be marked until the later OS maps at the end of the century.

Copper works were erected in 1772 near the old castle site and manufactured iron rods, bars, bolts for shipping and tin plates. The castle site was leased to the Caerleon Tin Master Mr John Butler, and was one of four tin-plate works in Monmouthshire, the others being Pontypool, Redbrook and Caerleon. There were two mills at the site, one powered by water, the other by steam. These were used to make puddled iron tin-bar. The bar and sheet rollings were sent to the Tydu Works for the final production of tinned sheets, along a tramway which ran through Tregwilym Fach Farm, farmed by William John Senior. The works are clearly shown on a number of Monmouthshire maps from this period.

The sale of the Tydu Estate appeared in the London Star in February 1806 and stated that the site was ideal in that it had a constant supply of water from the River Ebbw and access to the Sirhowy Tram Road. Rogerstone Works are shown on several maps thereafter and were long associated with the name of John Lewis & Co. The 1851 census states that the ironworks on the castle site employed thirteen people plus the ironmaster and was there until 1879. The increased demand for steel for railways and intense competition from America and Germany forced the works to close. It was not until 1885 that Nettlefolds steelworks came to the site.

Nettlefolds and GKN

The old Castle Works at Hadley, Shropshire were forced to close due to increasing costs and competition. Having been assured of a place in a new working community, the Shropshire men and their families came to Rogerstone in 1885 to a newly opened Nettlefolds. By 1887 the works was in full operation. In 1902 Nettlefolds merged with Guest, Keen & Co., the war years seeing their entire output used solely for the war effort. With the effect of the Depression being felt on the steel industry, steel was being imported from Cardiff to make their hot roll products. The cost of transporting the steel became too high and so it was decided to close down the old plants and build a new modern plant at Cardiff. By 1938 GKN at Rogerstone had closed. Incidentally, the name of the site, Castle Works, came from Shropshire – named after the first successful steel plant at Hadley Castle, Wellington, which included a Bessemer converter. The construction of this second plant took place under the supervision of Edward Steer, an appointee of Nettlefolds Company. The Rogerstone site being near the castle ruins was purely coincidental.

Northern Aluminium Company

With the threat of the Second World War, the Northern Aluminium Company was approached by the Air Ministry to supervise construction and management of an aluminium sheet and extrusion factory on behalf of the Government. The Rogerstone site was ideally located with its access to water and rail and plenty of labour available since GKN's closure. Work started on the site in 1939 and by 1944 a wide range of sections were being produced for the aircraft industry, in particular vast quantities of spar booms for the successful Spitfire aircraft.

Tydu House. An advertisement for the sale of the Tydu Estate, which appeared in the London Star of February 1806, describes this 'nearly completed dwelling house' which later became the home of John Lewis, manager of the Tin Works. Viscount Tredegar gave the house and land, about eleven-and-a-half acres, to the Parish of Rogerstone in 1927 on the understanding that a welfare scheme be carried out. The house was later demolished to make room for a new bypass to be built. The house was then replaced by a new hall and changing rooms.

The old steel works before demolition to make way for the building of the Alcan works, c. 1939.

Above: Workers from the Iron Works at the castle site, *c.* 1900.

Left: Girls employed in the GKN Nail Factory during the First World War. Top left: Beatrice Irving (*née* Hatherall), Bottom: Hannah Davies. In 1905 HP (Huggets Patent) Wire Nail Works was transferred from Birmingham to Rogerstone alongside the Steel Works and Rolling Mill. Nettlefolds became the largest manufacturer of wood screws in the world and supplied not only Britain but also the Empire (vast as it then was), according to J.C. Davies in *Industrial Development and Change,* a historical pamphlet celebrating Bethesda Chapel's 250th anniversary.

GUEST, KEEN & NETTLEFOLDS
Limited,

Castle Works, Rogerstone, near Newport, Mon.,
-- and --
Imperial Mills, Coverack Road, Newport, Mon.

MANUFACTURERS OF

At Castle Works--

STEEL BARS—ROUND, SQUARE, FLAT, HALFROUND, OVAL, Etc., FOR GENERAL PURPOSES
STEEL BARS—OF SPECIAL QUALITIES.
STEEL BARS—FOR USE IN FERRO CONCRETE CONSTRUCTION.
STEEL HOOPS OF SPECIAL QUALITIES & TEMPERS FOR WOOL BALING, COTTON BALING, CASING, BUNDLING & OTHER PURPOSES.
WIRE RODS OF VARIOUS DESCRIPTIONS AND QUALITIES
ROLLED WIRE FOR FENCING PURPOSES, Etc.
WIRE NAILS—ROUND, SQUARE, OVAL, TRIANGULAR CLOUT NAILS, FENCING STAPLES, TELEGRAPH STAPLES, PANEL PINS, Etc.

At Coverack Road--

BRIGHT DRAWN WIRE, "CASTLE" BRAND   TINMAN'S WIRE   COPPERED WIRE   BEST STEEL SPRING WIRE
BEST CHARCOAL WEAVING AND BINDING WIRE
BEST GALVANISED WEAVING AND BINDING WIRE
BEST TINNED WEAVING AND BINDING WIRE
BEST CRUCIBLE STEEL WIRE
GALVANISED STRAND WIRE.   GALVANISED WIRE CLOTHES LINES

☞ All enquiries, orders and correspondence to be addressed to: **Castle Works, Rogerstone, Newport, Mon.**

Advertisement for GKN from the *South Wales Argus* dated 14 July 1914. In 1902 Nettlefolds merged with Guest, Keen & Co. to become Guest, Keen & Nettlefolds (GKN). From 1914 to 1918 the Castle Works was entirely under the direction of the Ministry of Munitions, the output solely for the war effort.

GKN Staff, 1918-19. Back row, third from left: Charles Hodges. Back row, extreme right: Edgar Bailey. Middle row: James Jones, Herbert Jones, James Williams, John Corfield. Front row centre: Doris Marks, Terry Thomas.

This photograph was taken at the front of the GKN Castle Works Institute in 1926. The top two rows are Trade Union Representatives of that time. The front row shows employees with more than fifty years service. From left to right, top row: William Worral, Ted Beddow, George Hatherall, Enoch Watkins, Harry Morgan, Reg Thomas, Ted Fletcher, Charles Evans. Middle row: George Groucott, Ted Taylor, Walter Power, Harry Harrison, Sid Phelps, Dick Lloyd, William Thomas, Tom Rees. Front Row: Sam Fletcher, Jess Fletcher, George Hampton, Sam Forgham, John Jones, William Dyke, Enoch Archer.

The ironworks site being cleared ready for the construction of the Aluminium works (east). In the background can be seen The Buildings, Rogerstone Hotel, The Nook, and fields on which various stages of housing estates were built. The viaduct into the works can be clearly seen and also the works offices.

The threat of war in 1939 worked to the advantage of industry in Rogerstone. The Northern Aluminium Company were approached by the Air Ministry to supervise construction of and manage an aluminium sheet and extrusion factory on behalf of the British Government. Rogerstone already had a site, which could be used, and there was plenty of labour available since the departure of GKN, plus the railway link was still in place. Building started in August 1939, just weeks before war was declared. Builders arrived from Oxford and forward planners from Banbury. Staff and workers from Alcan's Banbury site were brought in initially with local people being taken on from September 1939. By 1940 production of aluminium had begun and was leaving Rogerstone by rail and lorry for aircraft factories in Southampton and the Midlands. It was used to make wings and bodies of Spitfires, Hurricanes, Lancaster Bombers and other aeroplanes needed for the war.

Visit by Sir Stafford Cripps, Minister of Aircraft Production, 20 March 1943. The number of workers coming to the village increased greatly and they had a large canteen on the works site at the Institute, where they also had pep talks from RAF personalities.

The East works, looking north, October 1941. All buildings were camouflaged so that from the air they looked like countryside. All buildings were sealed tight so that no light was visible from the air.

Alcan during the Second World War.

During the 1940s 8,000 people were employed at the Aluminium Works. Half of these were women who replaced the men who were now in the armed forces. They had to operate presses, cranes and trucks exactly as the men had done.

An aerial view of the new strip mill, *c*. 1951. By the end of the decade the course of the river behind the works had changed.

A new mill was opened to meet the increasing demands for aluminium. It was one third of a mile long, Europe's largest continuous strip mill, and covered seven and a half acres. It was one of the largest aluminium covered buildings in the world.

River Ebbw diverted in Noral works expansion scheme
By *South Wales Argus* Industrial Reporter, 16 September 1958

To make way for further expansion to their giant works at Rogerstone, the Northern Aluminium Company Limited are at present diverting the course of the River Ebbw. Within the next few days the river as it flows through the parish of Rogerstone will take a completely new course. For a quarter of a mile it will follow a channel made by man, eventually its old bed will be filled in and lost. By straightening the river as it meanders past the west boundary of the works, the company will gain about seven acres, on which a new productive plant can be installed.

For several weeks past the earth moving equipment of the contractors, G. Percy Trentham Ltd of Cardiff, have been spraying out a new 65ft wide riverbed – several feet wider than the old one. Bulldozers and scrapers, operating in a sea of mud caused by the heavy rains, have been carving out the main channel, while draglines have been trimming the banks. A dam has been left at each end of the channel to contain the river, which is now running higher than normal, and in the last stage of the operation, which is expected to take place on Wednesday or Thursday, these will be demolished and the river will take its new course. Filling of the old bed will take place later. (Reproduced by kind permission of the *South Wales Argus*)

Cutting the new course for the River Ebbw.

The new course of the River Ebbw after completion.

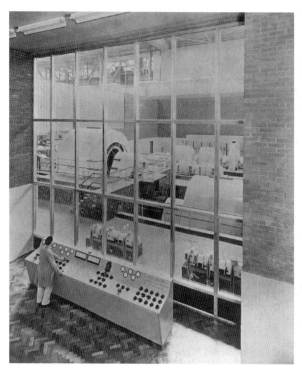

A view of the 144-in mill motor room seen from the gallery of the control room. Before the huge aluminium framed window is the control room console.

Below: The screwdown and exciter generator set for 144-in mill.

Opposite, below: East Works Extrusion 'A' shift, 1970s.

Part of the motor room for the 144-in mill, with drive motors in the background.

An aerial photograph from Tydu showing the expanse of the works, *c.* 1950. The Welfare Grounds Cricket pitch can be seen in the foreground. Note the house on the bottom left of the photograph, behind the school. This was knocked down when the bypass was built.

In 1947, Northern Aluminium purchased the land from the Government under the umbrella of Alcan Aluminium Co. Ltd. They also purchased other surrounding and bordering land until by 1950 the whole site from east to west had been acquired and occupied by the works. John's Farm and the allotments rapidly disappeared.

Above, left: Clifford Butler, shunter at Alcan Works, August 1957. *Above, right:* Clifford Butler in the engine sheds.

Left: Demob papers for Clifford Butler.

Clifford Butler was born in 1895 and lived in Viaduct Place with his parents, William and Elizabeth, where he continued to live after his marriage to Mary Esther Small, until the late 1930s. He was in the Monmouth Regiment in 1914 and served in France between 1915 and 1918. He was demobbed in March 1919. He later worked as a train driver for the Alcan works until his retirement.

Rogerstone Power Station in 1991. This was the first power station to be completely built by the South West Division of CEGB since nationalisation of the electricity industry and was built in response to the ever increasing demands of the industrial consumers of the area. At this time electricity was being imported from England!

Rogerstone was third choice for the site; Llanover and Machen were rejected after objections in both areas. Despite protests from Rogerstone Parish Council and a public enquiry, the Minister of Fuel and Power gave consent for the erection of the power station at Rogerstone and work commenced on the site in September 1954. Sir Christopher Hinton, Chairman of the Board of CEGB, officially opened the power station on 30 October 1958. The power station cost £7 million to build and covered ninety-two acres. The power station was decommissioned in 1984, but not demolished until September 1991.

In 1989 development plans for the site were already under discussion. The plans were for a village and business park with access to the site from the new Risca bypass. After several delays in plans the *South Wales Argus* dated 22 January 1999 reports that planning permission for 355 homes on the former Rogerstone Power Station site had been granted. The village continues to grow.

Demolition of the cooling towers, September 1991.

The demolition of the chimney and towers by explosion was witnessed by hundreds of people along any and every vantage point.

Left: Smoke at the top of the chimney shows where the charges were set.

Below, left and right: The chimney starts to topple.

two

Canal and
Railway

The Canal

In 1792 the Monmouthshire Canal opened and received its parliamentary Act. The Newport to Crumlin arm was the most challenging and so the last section to be completed. When this opened in 1798 it firmly placed the Cefn on the map.

The Fourteen Locks section at Rogerstone was the last section to be completed, rising 168ft within half a mile. Labour for the construction of the canal was provided by local farmers and villagers, but also by navvies from Somerset, Cardiganshire and Carmarthenshire. So the influx of incomers commenced.

The canal bed had to be lined with a watertight seal, which was a mixture of loam and clay. This was puddled and spread over the bottom and sides to a depth between 18 and 36in. Sometimes cattle or sheep were driven along the bed of the canal to assist in the puddling process. The fourteen locks were arranged in seven pairs. Each lock drained into a side pond, saving the water for the next time the chamber below was filled. The engineer of this impressive piece of canal engineering was Thomas Dadford Junior.

Since not all sites were accessible by water, an Act allowed for a number of tram roads to be built, linking up with the canals. By the 1830s, at the height of activity on the canal, the Monmouthshire Canal Co. owned over forty miles of tramways. Unfortunately the coming of the railways meant the decline in use of the canals for transportation and in 1848 the canal owners changed their name to the Monmouthshire Railway & Canal Co. The last barge on the canal was in 1930.

The locks have received much needed attention and restoration over the years. An interpretation centre built there in 1978 explains the history of the locks and the Monmouthshire Canal system. Work is ongoing, thanks to the Monmouthshire Brecon & Abergavenny Canal Trust and supporting groups.

The Railway

The growth of the iron and coal industries was instrumental in the coming of the railway through Rogerstone – the canal alone unable to cope with the amount of traffic. The railway system was born from the tram roads connecting the waterways to the industries. December 1829 saw the first steam engine introduced to the area when *Britannia* made its first journey from Tredegar to Newport. By 1845 the Canal Navigation Co. was responsible for the conversion of the Western Valley Line to the new standard gauge. In 1848 The Monmouthshire Railway & Canal Co. as it was now known, was given authority to carry passengers. The first signal posts were erected at Tydu Station in December 1850 and the railway was opened for passengers and parcels. In August 1875 the Monmouthshire Railway & Canal Co. leased their undertaking to Great Western Railways, fully amalgamating in 1880. In 1887 there were six trains a day in both directions every weekday and two trains on a Sunday. The name of the station was changed from Tydu to Rogerstone in 1898.

The start of the vast sidings complex began in 1885, with links to the Castle Works being added, over a viaduct on lower Tregwilym Road in 1888. More lines were added in 1890 and further expansion took place in the 1920s so that Rogerstone became a notable marshalling yard for coal trains. As road transport took over the railway declined and passenger transport had ceased completely, in both the Western and Eastern Valleys of Gwent, by 1962. Rogerstone station closed completely when the goods yard closed in November 1966. The marshalling yards finally closed in 1968. The Ebbw Rail Campaign is hoping to bring passenger services back through Rogerstone with the Ebbw Vale to Cardiff line. A new station is planned for Rogerstone near the new Afon Village on the old power station site.

Between 1802 and the 1830s trade on the canal increased tremendously. It could take up to two hours to steer a barge through the locks when it was busy.

Pensarn Pound, 1963. Pensarn was the lock-keepers cottage where a Mr Jack Brooks lived from 1919, working on the canal even though boats no longer used it.

The Canal, Newport.

An early view of the canal at Fourteen Locks.

The rise of the canal can be seen in this photograph taken from Allt-yr-yn.

Above: Bill Tippins, who worked on the canal for thirty-six years as a 'lengthman'. This meant he was responsible for a particular length of the canal. He lived with his family at Canalside Cottage.

Left: The children on the raft are John and Sylvia Tippins, children of Bill. The raft on which they are playing is actually Bill's workboat, which he would use to check on his length of canal.

Rogerstone railway station, 8 July 1957.

The derelict ruins of Rogerstone station, *c.* 1970. A single line is all that remains.

Above: Rogerstone Hump shunting, 8 June 1957. The Hump was a raised section of track, which allowed the wagons to gravitate into different sidings, to be formed into trains for dispatch country wide.

Left: Access was provided to the newly built power station in 1957, but the railway ceased to be used, with coal imports then being brought in by road.

An aerial view of lower Tregwilym Road, which shows the extensive marshalling yards on the right.

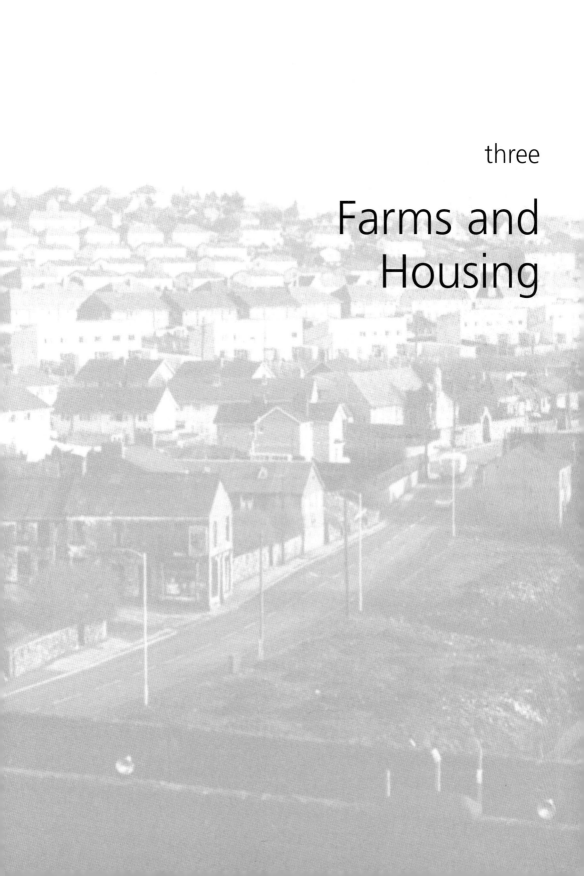

three

Farms and
Housing

Farms

The 1844 tithe map shows that Rogerstone was essentially an agricultural district with small pockets of industry at Tydu and Tregwilym, much of the land belonging to the Tredegar Estates. Tregwilym Farm, which was then occupied by John Morgan and owned by Phillip Jones, was 192 acres. It was eventually demolished to make way for the expansion of the marshalling yards and is now part of the bypass. In 1879 the Tredegar Estate acquired Tregwilym Fach Farm, in liquidation, from Mary Thomas Lewis for £1,700. Croesllanfro in 1700 was recorded as a farmstead, garden and twenty Welsh acres leased to John Morgan for £10 a year 'and a suit of mill'. The farm is entered on the 1844 map and tithe apportionments belonging to Cross William Bros when it was part of the Tredegar Estates covering 161 acres and occupied by Phillip Rees. Cwm Farm was also acquired by the Tredegar Estates, but quite late on, in 1901. In the 1882 *John's Directory for Newport and Neighbourhood*, there are eighteen farms listed under Rogerstone. Many of the farms have been swallowed up by development, Tregwilym Fach, The Wern, High Cross and Blackbird's Nest to name a few, the street or road name the only clues to their existence. A few farms remain on the outskirts, such as the Mount Pleasant Farms, Wenallt and Golynos, but on a much smaller scale, with new housing developments encroaching on the land yearly.

Housing

In 1844 the most densely populated areas were the lower end of Tregwilym Road and an area on the Cefn around the present day Rising Sun Public House. According to the electoral registers, apart from farms and individually named houses, the following streets existed prior to 1888: Bethesda Row (1848/9), Bethesda Place (1856), London Row, Viaduct Place (1856), Ebenezer Terrace (1870) and Tregwilym Road (1870 – although there were no houses on the library side of the road until the 1890s) and Victoria Gardens (1886). In 1887, with the coming of Nettlefolds, the Rogerstone House Property and Investment Co. Ltd built a large number of three-bedroomed workmen's cottages forming James, Edwin and Charles Street, known locally as 'the New Buildings' or 'the Buildings'. These houses were all in close proximity to the works.

The period 1887-90 saw the building of a great many homes for the Nettlefolds workers who had come down from Shropshire. On the south side of the viaduct, John, Hadley, Wellington and McLean Streets were built. Nettlefolds Terrace and Rogerstone Terrace were also built during this period, along with Orchard Terrace and Orchard Place, Woodland Terrace, Albert Terrace on Risca Road and Victoria Terrace.

The building of houses along the upper part of Tregwilym Road began in earnest as prosperity grew and key workers chose well-built spacious homes. Individual house names appeared on the electoral registers until 1951 when Tregwilym Road was completely renumbered. The building of the Uplands, St John's Road (now Church Street) and Park

Tregwilym Fach Farm, known locally as 'John's Farm', now the entrance to the Alcan car park. In 1876 this farm was occupied by William John and remained in the John family until the 1950s when Alcan bought up the land surrounding the works. This photograph was taken from a house opposite on Tregwilym Road, probably in the 1930s.

Avenue began at the end of the First World War, with St John's Crescent, Wern Terrace and Ifor Hael Road being completed before the end of the 1920s. The development of the High Cross area began in the 1930s, continuing into the post-war years. Thornbury Park and Cefn Wood Estate were built later on to accommodate the residents from The Nook and the New Buildings when these houses were eventually demolished. Much of that area is now taken up with the bypass. Court Gardens and Thornhill are mentioned in the 1930 directories, but were market gardens at this time. The development of these areas for housing began in the early 1970s. Formerly the site of prefabs built after the war, Oak Road houses were built in 1970-71, along with the three-storey flats. Rogerstone continues to grow with further developments on the former power station site and at Great Oaks Park. What was once two small hamlets is now a desirable locality on the outskirts of the city of Newport.

Above, left: Sale of Golynos Farm, 1876. *Above, right:* Particulars of Sale for the sale of Golynos Farm.

The Golynos Oak

Residents of Rogerstone will be familiar with the name Oak, it occurring in the names of streets, old and existing public houses and several residential houses in the area. The name Oak is believed to have derived from the magnificent Golynos Oak, the largest oak tree ever to be felled in Britain according to national records.

The tree is said to have had a trunk that measured 9ft 7in in diameter, six of its main limbs each the size of a normal oak tree. It was a popular site for tourists and picnic parties in the late eighteenth century, but unfortunately, its popularity was its downfall. The owners of the estate on which the tree stood were exasperated by constant trespassers and so decided to have it felled. Mr Thomas, a supplier of timber to the dockyard at Portsmouth, purchased the oak for one hundred guineas. It took five men twenty-one days to fell the tree and a further one-hundred-and-twenty-eight days to convert it to timber. It yielded over three tons of bark, and 2,426 cubic feet of timber. Curiously, a 10lb stone was found at the very centre of its trunk, where it had lain for 500 years. The timber was largely used for the building of ships for the Royal Navy. Mr English of Bath, who was a master cabinet-maker, bought the remaining root timber for the sum of one hundred guineas. The beautifully grained wood was used for fine tables, wardrobes and bookcases. One of the tables is said to have been acquired by Lady Llanover of Gwent.

Eventually Capt. Phillips built a house on the site where the tree had stood and named the house Derwen Fawr, which translates to Great Oak' and is now the clubhouse of the Newport Golf Club.

Opposite: Reproduction from the 1883 Ordnance Survey map with kind permission of the Ordnance Survey.

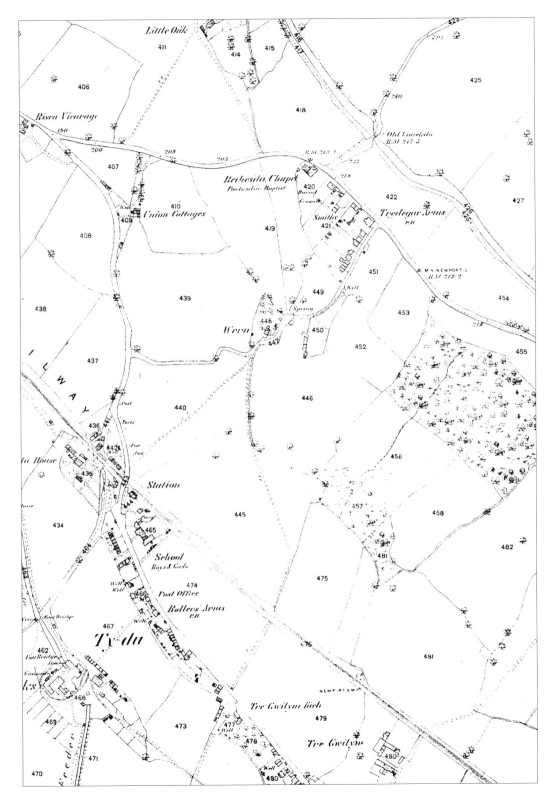

Little Oak

411

414   415

417

406   425

418   280

Risca Vicarage   Old Lanelein
190   B.M 217·5

200   209   203   B.M 213·1

407   427

Bethesda Chapel
Particular Baptist   420   422

410   Tredegar Arms
409   Union Cottages   419   Smithy   P.H

408   421

439   449   451   B.M 273·2

438   453   454

446   Spring

Wern   450   452   455

447

I L W A Y   437

440   446   456

436   Post

H House   443   445   457   458

436   Station   481   482

434   465

School
Boys & Girls   475

474
Post Office

466

Rollers Arms
P.H.

467   481

Ty du

462
Foot Bridge

468   NEWPORT 3 M

469   473   477   Tre Gwilym fach   479

478   Tre Gwilym

471   480

470   480

41

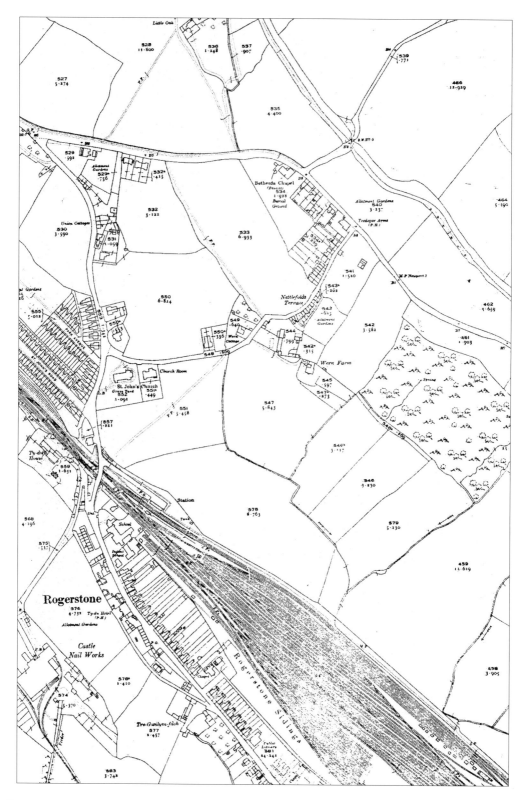

Hadley Street before demolition in the early 1970s.

Wellington Street in the early 1970s. Wellington and Hadley Streets were so named as reminders of Shropshire for those workers who came to Rogerstone with the opening of the new steel works in the late nineteenth century.

Opposite: Reproduction from the 1920 Ordnance Survey map with kind permission of the Ordnance Survey. The development of Tregwilym Road and the Cefn is seen on these maps, as is the extent of the marshalling yards.

McLean Street in the early 1970s. On 17 December 1887, the *South Wales Echo* reported that 'Mr John MaClane, property owner and builder from Rogerstone, was summoned by the rural sanitary authority for allowing cottages to be occupied before notice had been given by the sanitary authority, and also neglecting to provide proper sanitary ventilations to the new buildings'. In his defence Mr MaClane said the demand for houses in Rogerstone was so great that people took possession of the properties against his will and would not leave when asked. He knew there were up to eight families lodging together. He was fined 20s and was told he would be liable to a further fine of £5 and a daily penalty of 10s if the tenants did not leave.

John Street in the early 1970s. These four streets made up St John's Square, affectionately known as The Nook. It consisted of much smaller two-bedroomed houses for those less well paid. The roads here were composed of coal fire ashes that caused dust in the summer and black puddles in winter.

Rogerstone Terrace, *c.* 1920. The two ladies are standing outside Rowland's, the drapers shop.

An advertising page that appeared in an Eisteddfod pamphlet in 1926, which includes an advertisement for Rowland's, the drapers. Mr Rowland was also the Registrar of Births and Deaths for Rogerstone sub-district. Hiley, the butchers was also found in the 1901 Monmouthshire Directory where it also lists Mr Hiley as a boot and shoe maker and the Sub-Post Master.

45

Right: An advertisement found in the 1926 Eisteddfod pamphlet for Periam's. Periam's, the brush-makers are mentioned in *Kelly's 1901 Monmouthshire Directory*.

The 1901 Monmouthshire directory shows Tydu as having a stationer and lamp dealer, a number of boot and shoe repairers, hairdressers, several grocers and butchers shops, a draper, brush-makers and two market gardeners.

Below: Watkins' Stores can also be found listed in *Kelly's 1901 Monmouthshire Directory*. This advertisement, from a 1926 Eisteddfod pamphlet, shows the business was still going strong.

85

'Phone—18, Rhiwderin.   Established 1894.

THE OLD FIRM— J. PERIAM,

Grocer, Provision Merchant, Coal Merchant, and Wholesale Brush Maker.

1, 2, 3, John St., Rogerstone.

Home-Cured Bacona Speciality.

All kinds of Brushes Made to Order.

Our Motto - "QUALITY."

HERBERT L. PERIAM,

TREGWILLYM STORES

– AND POST OFFICE, –

Rogerstone, Mon.

Palethorpe's Cooked Ham, Brawn, Sausage, Pies.	GROCER AND CONFECTIONER	China, Hardware, Stationery &c.

WATKINS' STORES,

Grocers and Provision Merchants.

TREGWILLYM ROAD, ROGERSTONE.

FOR BEST QUALITY GROCERIES.

„   BEST   „   PROVISIONS.

„   BEST   „   TEAS.

AT LOWEST PRICES ALWAYS.

PROMPT ATTENTION GIVEN ALL ORDERS,

also at 122, Commercial Street, Newport.

Tel. 3364.

Above: The chemist's shop, No. 254 Tregwilym Road. This was originally named Bristol House and was occupied by the Giles family from the early 1920s through to the late 1940s. It became known as the Pharmacy in the Electoral Register listings of the 1940s.

Left: The Midland Bank, Rogerstone Branch, No. 57 Tregwilym Road. This was formerly Hillman's sweet shop and prior to the re-numbering of Tregwilym Road was No. 5 Oak Tree Terrace. The site is now part of the Alcan car park opposite the library.

Lower Tregwilym Road after the demolition of The Nook.

The Viaduct, c. 1972. In 1888 GWR provided siding links with Castle Works and a stone viaduct
was built. The bridge was eventually demolished in June 1971 after being declared a traffic hazard.
The efforts to have it demolished were speeded up after a bus became stuck beneath the narrow
arch and twelve people were injured. Some of the stones from the demolished viaduct were used
in the building of the 'Castle' for the Ebbw Vale Festival in 1992.

Puddlers Row. These cottages can be found on the 1844 tithe map but date from earlier, having been occupied by the clay puddlers engaged in the building of the canal. Many years later the name was changed to School Terrace.

These cottages can be found on the 1883 OS map and were known as Shop Row. The post office and the old Tin-Plate school stood next to them and also a small shop that jutted out into the road, the site of which is now under development. The cottages are no longer called Shop Row but were re-numbered Nos 95-107 Tregwilym Road.

Rogerstone House was built for Edward Steer, an appointee of Nettlefolds, who supervised construction of the Rogerstone Nettlefolds plant. The house continued to be used by staff of the works and successors of the site. Today it houses Mandrake Associates Ltd.

Numbers 83-85 Tregwilym Road. These were originally three cottages, the two on the lane side having been knocked into one. A cottage and garden can be found on the tithe map and was owned by the Tredegar Estate. In 1844 William Rosser occupied it. The 1883 OS map clearly shows three cottages on this site. They were known as Tregwilym Place, being changed to Nos 83-87 Tregwilym Road in 1952.

The Nick, No. 156 Tregwilym Road, formerly the local police station for Rogerstone.

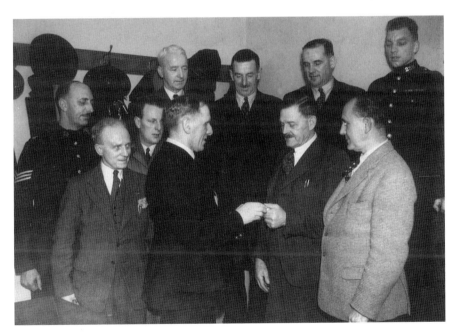

Superintendent A. Bowket of Risca Division, Monmouthshire Constabulary, presenting Special Constable H.G. Bailey of Rogerstone, with a long-service medal at Rogerstone police station. Other Special Constables to receive the long-service medal were G.T.W. Jones, (Rogerstone), A.E. Bolwell and R.J. Pobjoy (High Cross), and W. Knight (Machen). Also in the picture is Police Sergeant Poulson (Rogerstone).

A street party at Nettlefolds Terrace. The houses on the right of this photograph were built around 1889 and named Nettlefolds Terrace at the time. The houses are still there today but are now part of Bethesda Place.

The Blacksmith's shop on High Cross Road, known as the Cefn Smithy. This photograph from around 1930 shows Mr Edward Russell (centre), Champion Shoeing Smith.

four

Our Library

The Rogerstone Carnegie Library, *c.* 1906.

The Library

On 11 November 1905 the *County Observer and Monmouthshire Advertiser* carried a paragraph about the opening of the Carnegie library at Rogerstone on 4 November:

> FREE LIBRARY FOR ROGERSTONE – Lord Tredegar formally opened a free library at Rogerstone on Saturday afternoon. Some two years ago an appeal was made to Mr Carnegie, who gave £1,400 towards its erection. Lord Tredegar gave the site and, in his short address on Saturday, said he would be very pleased to present some books for the library to supplement the number they already had.

The *Weekly Argus* for the same date stated: 'Saturday last will be remembered as one of the red-letter days in the history of Rogerstone'.

The inhabitants of Rogerstone turned out en-masse for the opening ceremony performed by Lord Tredegar. The initial sum of £1,000 offered by Mr Carnegie towards the cost of the library was increased to £1,400 after intervention from Mr Edward Steer, managing director of Guest, Keen & Nettlefolds Ltd and another gentleman of Mr Carnegie's acquaintance. The accommodation provided a reading room, a library with lending and reference departments and librarians' rooms. It was to open on weekdays from 10am to 10pm and the lending department to open once a week. The reading room was situated at the rear of the building where the British Legion's Rogerstone Roll of Honour can be found on the wall.

Mr Artemus Llewellyn, chairman of the Rogerstone Parish Council, said how fortunate they were to have such a magnificent building and that today was the summit of their success as they had 'always had in view an institution of that sort' for the last ten years or more. On 11 November 1905, the *Weekly Argus* reported that Llewellyn:

> hoped it would not only prove a boon to the present generation, but to those who were living after they had gone. He hoped that as time went on and Rogerstone continued to prosper, the library shelves would be well stocked with good and useful books, and with this object in view the Council must continue to husband their resources and procure the best books available.

Lord Tredegar was thanked profusely 'for the great amount of good that he had done in the hamlet of Rogerstone in the past'.

Prior to the building of the library the schools at Tydu had been used as a free library and reading rooms in connection with the Parish Council and contained 700 volumes.

Early in 1941 the Rogerstone Parish Council were approached and asked for their help to set up a British Restaurant. The public library service was suspended in order to grant use of the premises as a British Restaurant subject to reinstatement of the premises within six months of the end of occupancy or the end of the war. The agreement dated 11 December 1941 stated that the premises should continue to be available for library purposes from 4pm each day and the book-issuing room be available from 2.30pm each Friday for the purpose of payment of pensions to former employees of GKN. Sir Charles Edwards, CBE, Member for Bedwellty opened the British Restaurant, Rogerstone, at 12pm on 5 May 1942. Over 1,300 British Restaurants were catering for the needs of the public in wartime, helping poor people to get meals which otherwise might be beyond their means. In 1944 a pensioner had to pay 6d for a complete midday meal. Children of the nearby school also used the British Restaurant to have dinners since they had no school canteen facilities. This led to a dispute between the Parish Council and the District Council when in 1945 the Restaurant Committee deferred closing the British Restaurant until a school canteen was provided. The Parish Council felt that the people of Rogerstone had been deprived of their library service for long enough and formerly requested that the premises be restored to them on 31 July 1945. The dispute continued and the British Restaurant remained open until 1947. A schedule dated February 1947 details the costs to repair damage caused while the building was used a British Restaurant and for necessary redecoration at a total cost of £208 11s.

The building also housed the local Registrar's Office, which was situated in one of the small offices on the left hand side of the building, which were knocked through when the library was refurbished in 1993.

In 1991 the library was threatened with closure but residents and councillors signed a petition calling for the library to remain open, as they believed it was part of the town's heritage. Repairs and complete refurbishment were carried out at the end of the 1992/93 financial year and the library was re-opened on 17 May 1993 by the Mayor of Newport, Cllr Alan Perry.

'This is a community library in the true sense of the word, mindful of its history and held in high regard by the local population,' is how an article in the *South Wales Argus* on 17 May 1993 described it.

On 23 July 2003 the library became a Grade II listed building. It is described as a 'well-designed small Edwardian library building in free classical style'. The library building's existence is at least assured for the present time when so many of the village's older buildings are being lost to redevelopment.

Left and above: The interior of the library in 1990 as it was before refurbishment. The entire library was housed in what is now the Adult section. The Junior section was once a series of small offices, one of which was used by the Registrar of the district in past years.

Opposite, below: Face painting at the Teddy Bears' Picnic.

Above: The Children's Librarian, reading a story at the Teddy Bear's Picnic held at Rogerstone Library on 31 July 1990. The library has held numerous events, including themed evenings, talks by various authors, children's story times and even a bouncy castle and Teddy Bears' Picnic in its own garden.

The British Legion Rogerstone Roll of Honour. The 1914–18 illuminated War Memorial was originally fitted on the east side of the British Legion Memorial Hall at Rogerstone. In 1960 the Memorial was removed to the Carnegie Public Library when the British Legion Club became a licensed premises. A new memorial plaque for the two wars was unveiled in October 1961 by Dr George Hull, JP and dedicated by Canon Ivor Phillips of St Paul's, Newport. The illuminated Memorial is kept undercover for protection, the cover being removed each year for the Remembrance Day Service held in the library. In 1993 when refurbishment of the library took place a photographic replica was produced which hangs on the wall next to the original.

five

Public Houses

OLD GLOBE INN

The Licensed Trade

The removal of restrictions by the 1838 Beer-house Act brought into being beer retailers who kept beerhouses or beer shops which could only sell beer or cider. For the price of two guineas anyone could set up a beerhouse. Quite often a room in a house was set aside from which to sell beer, the owners seeking to supplement their income. This may account for the number of 'pub' names, which appeared and disappeared within short spaces of time, most reverting back to normal dwelling houses. There are very few areas with licensing records for beer shops before 1872.

On a list of licenses granted by magistrates in the parish of Bassaleg in 1811 the High Cross Inn is mentioned. It was located at the top of High Cross Lane, approximately where the garage is presently located. The 1841 census names Rachel Rosser, aged seventy-four, as the publican. Philip Rosser, aged forty-five, is also recorded there and his occupation is farmer. The tithe records show the land was owned by Sir Charles Morgan and included High Cross public house. The inn appears on registers until 1875, after which time only the farm is listed.

The earliest entry I could find that mentions the Rising Sun by name was in 1871. The King William IV was a canal-side inn on the Cefn, on the opposite side of the road to the Rising Sun, having access to both canal and road. It was owned by Sir Charles Morgan and appears on the 1841 census showing Hannah Jones as publican and remained in the Jones family until the mid-1920s. It is said to have been visited by the Chartists marching to Newport in 1839. It is still there today but has reverted to being a dwelling.

The newest pub in the area is The Oak Stave on Ruskin Avenue. This was originally built to take advantage of trade from the nearby Asda stores which opened in 1973. The Tredegar Arms at the top of Bethesda Place was first mentioned in *Slater's Directory of Monmouthshire* for 1858/9 when John Walters was listed there. The pub is still there today. The Old Globe at Tydu is also shown on the tithe map and the 1841 census. At the top of Tregwilym Road there was a pub called The Rollers Arms, this is listed as early as 1851 when Thomas Williams and his wife Blanch ran it. In 1889 Christopher Griffiths is listed at a property called the Rollers Hotel and in 1890 it appears as the Tydu Hotel. The Oak Tree inn was located near the present day entrance to Alcan. The first recorded entry was found in the 1871 census showing the occupier as being David Thomas, age fifty-three, employed at the Tin Mill. Rogerstone Hotel was built in 1887 with the coming of Nettlefolds to Rogerstone and was used by visitors to the Castle Works. The Royal Oak inn was located on the Newport side of the viaduct on lower Tregwilym Road. In 1861 George Highley was innkeeper. Entries appear in the electoral registers until 1967. Myrtle Grove is mentioned as far back as the 1844 tithe map, but it is not until 1865 that it is mentioned in connection with beer retailing, and then Mrs Margaret Benjamin is listed as beer retailer. In 1888 Myrtle Grove inn is listed under the name Rees Walters.

I will just mention briefly three inns found in Pye Corner as they have been covered in local history books on Bassaleg. Firstly The Three Horseshoes which had also been granted a magistrate's license in 1811 and is found on the 1841 census occupied by Edmund Thomas. The Three Salmons, at the opposite side of Pye Corner to The Three Horseshoes, is first found in 1882 occupied by Margaret Jones. It is still there today. The other pub found on that small 'island' was The Bush, located on the lower road below the Three Horseshoes. Other pubs mentioned in Rogerstone included The Puddlers Arms – 'adjoining the Tin Plate School'; the 1851 census mentions the Forge Hammer and also the Greyhound Inn; the 1855/56 electoral registers lists the Union Tavern under the name of David Williams of Rogerstone; the New Globe inn which first appeared in 1871 continued until 1909 after which time I found no further mention. In 1811 a license was also granted to Thomas Anthony of the Kevan (Cefn) and in 1815 the name Navigation House is found alongside his name on the license. This may be the public house marked on the 1844 tithe map that was located on the Rising Sun side of the Cefn but further along in the direction of Risca.

Friendly Society leaflet dated 1823 for High Cross. Friendly Societies received official recognition in the late eighteenth century during a time of social and industrial revolution. They were closely connected with public houses and some were named after their chosen meeting place. There was such a society that met at High Cross Inn. A member would be covered for accidents, sickness and burial; receive a pension in old age and know his widow and children would receive assistance in event of his death.

RULES AND ORDERS,

OF A

SOCIETY

OF

Tradesmen and Others,

Held at the dwelling house of

PHILIP ROSSER,

KNOWN BY THE NAME OR SIGN OF THE

HIGH CROSS,

SITUATE

IN THE PARISH OF BASSALEG,

In the said County.

———

NEWPORT:

Printed by John Partridge, High Street.

———

1823.

The old Rising Sun building with the tip of the new building in the top left hand corner. The 1861 census shows Rising Sun Cottages, but it is not until 1871 that the Rising Sun inn is mentioned.

The Rising Sun was rebuilt in about 1928 when the Davies family were the occupiers. The old building was demolished and the area is now part of the front car park.

King William IV public house on the canal bank, with the landlady Mary Jones and her granddaughter Francis in the early 1900s. Mrs Jones was the licensee from 1900 to around 1923. The license over the door reads: 'King Wm IVth, Mary Jones Licensed Retailer of Beer & Porter. To be consumed on the premises'.

The Tredegar Arms is one of the oldest public house buildings in Rogerstone, others having been rebuilt over the years or reverted to dwellings. Roger Morgan, the great-great-grandson of Abraham Morgan who was licensee from 1878-1900, took this photograph in the winter of 1984.

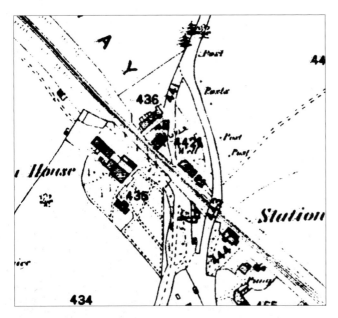

The Old Globe Inn on the 1883 OS map. This map shows the original position of the building in the piece of land behind that marked 442, moving forward to its present position when it was rebuilt in 1906.

The Old Globe Inn is shown on the 1844 tithe map as being owned by Sir Charles Morgan and occupied at that time by a Samuel Rosser. In later years the inn was said to be frequented by railway people since it was directly next to the railway line and near the station.

The Tydu Hotel occupied the site of the former Rollers Arms, which was included on the 1851 census. The inn changed its name in 1890 under the occupation of William Griffiths. This large building was demolished in the 1970s.

The Oak Tree was situated on Tregwilym Road where the present day entrance to Alcan is located. Richard Draper is the last recorded occupier in 1955, after which time Alcan bought up surrounding land, demolishing the inn and nearby cottages and farm.

In 1966, while under the management of William and Lillian Thomas, the name was changed from The Rogerstone Hotel to The Jolly Roger, as it was no longer used as a hotel. When the bypass was built, many of the streets surrounding the hotel were knocked down and the main road diverted. In November 2003 the building once more underwent a change of name and is now the British Raj, an Indian Restaurant.

The Royal Oak, No. 60 Tregwilym Road, which was on the Newport side of the viaduct. The name Crabb can just be seen on the sign – the Crabb family were there from 1910 through to the late 1920s. The inn appeared in the electoral registers until 1967.

The Myrtle Grove. The Benjamin family were occupiers of these premises from as early as 1844 and it probably started off as a beerhouse. The 1871 census lists there a Mrs Margaret Benjamin, aged seventy-one, widow, beerhouse keeper. The inn remained there until the 1970s, when it was demolished to make way for the bypass. The name is still retained in the name of the road Myrtle Drive leading onto a small housing estate next to the bypass and Myrtle Close which leads off the main road through the estate.

An aerial view of Pye Corner. The Bush public house can be seen on the left of the lower road and Bassaleg Junction signal box on the right.

The house immediately behind the present-day garage at Pye Corner was once the Three
Horseshoes. It continued as a public house until at least 1889 but after this date I could find no
mention of it in local directories. Like the King William IV, it has reverted to a dwelling.

The Bush was located on the lower part of Pye Corner with the Sirhowy Tram Road running
directly behind it.

six

Religion

Religion in Rogerstone

The earliest church in Rogerstone was the Baptist chapel at Bethesda on the Cefn. The building, which was originally a barn, was opened in 1742, the conversion work and much of the materials given freely by the congregation. Many of the old maps from this period have a 'Meeting Place' marked on them at the Cefn.

Ebenezer Chapel is found marked on the 1844 tithe map. It was situated on lower Tregwilym Road on the site where the Chapelwood Surgery was eventually built.

The coming of Nettlefolds and their Shropshire workforce was the instigation for other churches to be built in Rogerstone much later on. Lord Tredegar gave the land for the building of a church for the Anglicans at the top of the village. St John's church was opened in 1888 at a cost of £2,370. At around the same time a church was built for the Methodists lower down on Tregwilym Road. The religious revival at the time meant that soon the Wesleyan Methodist church was no longer big enough for its congregation and so plans for a new church were discussed in 1905. Lord Tredegar laid the foundation stone for the church on 2 August 1906. Again the congregation carried out much of the work. In 1969 the church was up for sale, the congregation having moved to a new Methodist church off Western Valley Road, taking with them the foundation stone laid by Lord Tredegar. In 1998 the church was demolished and is now the site of four houses. The Primitive Methodist's original chapel was situated on Tregwilym Road, off the lane at the end of Orchard Terrace or the 'Fourteen Houses' as they were known. It is now the site of the Pentecostal church. In 1935 the Wesleyans and Primitive Methodists joined together. Church outings and picnics were very popular on occasions such as Easter and Whitson Bank Holidays. During the Depression years the Primitive Methodists in Rogerstone were well known for their musical shows, pageants and eisteddfodau. Bethesda Baptist Mission located on lower Tregwilym Road was demolished with The Nook and rebuilt in Thornbury Park, eventually becoming independent, now known as the Cefn Wood Baptist church.

The Roman Catholics celebrated Mass once a month at a small house on Pye Corner. The congregation became too large to accommodate and so it was decided to build a church in Rogerstone. SS Basil and Gwladys Roman Catholic church on lower Tregwilym Road opened in 1892. At High Cross a Mission Room was erected in 1933, followed by a permanent church hall in 1954. Work began on a permanent church early in 1958, with the dedication of St Anne's church taking place on 11 December 1958.

Bethesda Chapel. The original barn was enlarged in 1795 then rebuilt in 1843. The building was completely remodelled in 1900 and stood until its replacement in 1996.

The New Christian Centre, Bethesda Chapel.

Interior of the old Bethesda Chapel before it was demolished.

Presentation of souvenir Coronation Bibles, Sunday 31 May 1953.

Bethesda Sunday school Teachers, *c*. 1981.

Bethesda Sunday school teachers and pupils, *c*. 1981.

The commercial barges had to have a thorough cleaning before use for this purpose. The barge would set off from the canal bridge by the Golf Links up the canal to Risca.

The annual Sunday school outing on the canal from Rogerstone to Risca. Bethesda Sunday school organised boat trips on the canal at Whitsun from 1897 until 1911.

Above and below: Bethesda Baptist Chapel Sisterhood Anniversary Tea, 1957.

St John's church, *c.* 1906. When built the church was equipped with a baptistery, as baptism by total immersion was a feature of local life at that time. A Sunday school and parish room were added close to the church and opened in 1900.

A boundary wall and lychgate were added in 1901 and the walls extended to enclose the lower part of the churchyard in the 1920s.

The Primitive Methodist Chapel. The original chapel was a timber-frame structure with corrugated steel cladding; a tin chapel. The Primitive Methodists used it until the union of the Wesleyan and Primitive Methodists in the 1930s. After that time the Pentecostal congregations used it until a new larger brick building replaced it.

The Primitive Methodists at Whiteheads Sports Ground, c. 1921.

The Castle Works Institute where many shows were staged, 1926. The show was performed by members and children of the Primitive Methodist church. Mr and Mrs Bill Holland took the leading parts. Front row, extreme left is Joe Jones the musical director and conductor. Centre front is Cynthia Manley. Other members of the cast included Bill Harrison, George Hillman, Edgar Bullock, Jim Morgan, Stan Lewis, Rex Major, Gert Major, Nancy Hillman, Bessie Beddoe, Winnie Holland and Agnes Manley.

Opposite, above: Rogerstone Primitive Methodists Sunday school, Whitson March 1920 at St John's Crescent. Carrying the banner on the left is Percy Beddow and on the right George Hillman. The man in the trilby is Fred Manley and the man in the white trousers is Edgar Bullock.

Bethesda Sunday school, Whitsun March 1920, on lower Tregwilym Road. The Whitsun Sunday Marches showed the intense community spirit, as scholars and teachers from all the local Sunday schools, churches and chapels united in their march from The Uplands down to St John's Square. The youngest scholars rode through the village on horse-drawn wagons, which were then used by the various curates and pastors as platforms from which to speak to the assembly, before they went off to their separate churches for their Whitsun celebrations.

Pamphlet covers for the 1926 and 1928 Eisteddfod at Rogerstone.

The Golden Chain pageant performed at Rogerstone Methodist church, *c.* 1950. It was written by the Reverend and Mrs Old, pictured on the extreme left and right of this photograph respectively.

The old Wesleyan church, built in 1887-88 by Mr Martin the builder.

The Wesleyan church, Tregwilym Road. Messrs Branscombe & Sons built the new church directly in front of the old church: the old building being incorporated as a schoolroom. The enthusiastic congregation did much of the labouring. When no longer in use as a church it housed a dance school, auction rooms and later a video post-production centre named Editrim Ltd until it was demolished in 1998.

SS Basil and Gwladys Roman Catholic church, lower Tregwilym Road. The consecration of this church took place on 13 October 1892. The site of the church is said to be one third of a mile across the fields from St Basil's, Bassaleg and one third of a mile west of the ruins of Rogerstone Castle.

Ebenezer Chapel, lower Tregwilym Road. The 1844 tithe map shows an Independent Chapel marked on this site. The landowner was John Armitage and others. Ebenezer Chapel is clearly marked on the 1887 OS map situated next to Ebenezer Terrace on lower Tregwilym Road. The building was demolished in 1982, but the burial grounds are still in existence next to what is now Chapelwood Surgery.

seven

Education

School Life

The Tin Works was responsible, in 1859, for setting up a school in the village for the benefit of the children whose parents were employed there. This was located at the top of Tregwilym Road near the row of cottages, (the site now under development). The school remained in this location, becoming a British School in 1870 then a Board School in 1876, before relocating to a new building further along on the opposite side of the road the following year. This building is presently occupied by Dudley's, the shopfitters, who took over the site in 1979. The new Rogerstone and Henllis Board School was opened in 1877 with provision for 300 pupils. It was enlarged in 1889 for 600 pupils by erecting a new department for the infants, to the right of the original building. The Education Development Plan for the area in 1953 stated the Tydu 'buildings and site were defective' and 'modern accommodation was necessary'. There were plans for a new school to be built at Victoria Gardens, necessary clearance having been obtained from the Ministry of Agriculture to use the market garden site. The plan included a new infants, junior and nursery school. Despite these plans it was not until the mid-1970s that a new school was built on a site at Cefn Wood. As the High Cross area of Rogerstone developed a new school was built there in 1938. High Cross School was expanded in 1953 with a new building to house the juniors and provision for a nursery school adjacent to the existing school. Further development in the Mount Pleasant area led to the opening of a school on Ruskin Avenue. Mount Pleasant School was opened in 1975, originally built as an infants' school for about 90 pupils. It is now a popular Primary School with treble that amount of pupils.

Tydu Senior School took pupils up to the age of fifteen. In 1936 Bassaleg Secondary Grammar School (Upper School) was built and so some of the older children were able to attend there. In the late 1950s the Graig Secondary Modern School (Lower School) was added when the school expanded to incorporate Grammar, Technical and Modern Schools for a widening catchment area.

Rogerstone and Henllis Board School, *c.* 1891.

Class III, *c.* 1910.

Class IV, *c.* 1910.

Tydu Infants, *c.* 1925–30.

Tydu Girls' School 1928/29. From left to right, back row: Lilly Long, ? Davies, Nel Cromwell, Megan Morgan, Elsie Warren, Gladys Walters, Hazel Cresswell, -?-. Third row: -?-, Rita Bailey, ? Newnes, Doreen Huggins, Chris Musselwhite, Joan Edmunds, Betty Wattie, Linda Marks. Second row: Elsie Roden, Kath Peckover, ? Smith, Joan Groucott, Dorothy Dyer, Dulcie Hampton, Joyce Evans, Kath Dwyer. Front row: Edie Whitcombe, Nancy Jones, Margaret Worrall, Gert Evans, -?-, Eileen Whitcombe, Margarite Knowles.

Infants' class, c. 1930.

Tydu Boys, *c.* 1930. From left to right; back row: S. Morris, Glyn Shepherd, Peter Scott, Eric Jones, John Hughes, Jim Tyack, John Roberts, Peter Angove. Middle row: Sam Stanworth, Malcolm Langley, Lionel Baker, John Dixon, John Walsh, Raymond Beale, Ken Faulkner, Sid Vaughan. Front row: Bob Witchard, Vivian Davies, Peter Emlyn.

Tydu School class, 1939.

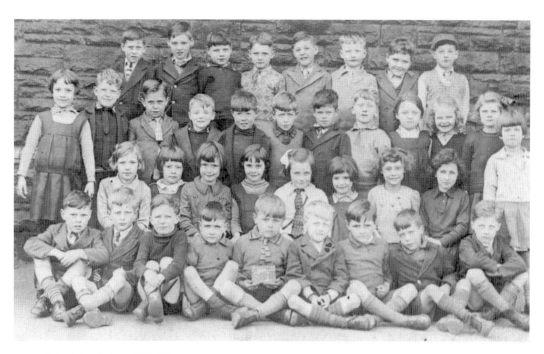

Tydu School class, 1939/40.

Tydu School class, 1944.

Tydu School class, *c.* 1946/47.

Rogerstone School, *c.* 1948. From left to right, back row: June Lee, Joyce Corbett, Gillian Evans, Marianne Price, Linda Lewis, Gill Powell, Margaret Bushell, Margaret O'Sullivan. Middle row: Peter Thomas, Ronald Fletcher, Alan Hatheral, Moira Maison, Moira James, Christine Cartwright, Sheila Richards, Gerald Roberts, Derek Picken, Michael Smith. Front row: Gordon Currier, Keith Sully, Tony Barnbrook, Allan Boxall (evacuee from London), John Edwards, Keith Howell, Raymond Jones, Gordon Hurley, Graham Warren.

Rogerstone School class, *c.* 1949.

Rogerstone School class, 1959. From left to right, back row: -?-, -?-, -?-, B. Stephen, T. Cornish,
R. Hancock, -?-, R. Allender, K. James. Third row: K. Gupwell, C. Fawkes, C. Powell, P. Herbert, -?-,
J. Burns. Second row: M. O'Connor, -?-, S. Luker, B. Bowden, D. Moss, P. Ray, M. Jenkins, ? Knox,
C. Sage, N. Coleman, C. Brown. Front row: A. Thomas, R. Moss, A. Davies, R. Morris, P. Tolley,
P. Hambleton, M. Williams, M. Jones.

High Cross School Football Team, 1963. From left to right, back row: Roger Panting, Keith Smith, Richard Beale, Anthony Hatherall, ? Pembridge. Middle row: Andre Claridge, Simon Williams, Neil Webb, Brian Williams, Anthony Arscott. Front row: Steven Thomas, David Williams, Keith Bevan.

The Fugitive Club, shown in the background, was used as a classroom because there was not enough room in the school. This photograph was taken by Mr Roy Scully, a teacher at High Cross School.

Tydu School, *c.* 1959.

Now offices for Dudley's, this is a photograph of the old school house, in 1984, which was home to the headmaster of Rogerstone and Henllis School in previous years.

High Cross Primary School class, 1944/45. From left to right; back row: Douglas Stephen, Geoffrey Pobjoy, Jacqueline Pritchard, Audrey West, Mary Dent, -?-, Bernard Minnett, Mr Percy Hallett. Third row: John Sach, Robert Bowen, Colin Barton, Norman Faulkner, Brian Harris, Brian Hodson, Billy John. Second row: Denise Selwood, Esme Brown, Margaret Hughes, Audrey Parfitt, Shirley Parfitt, Bunty Jobbins, Janet Colley, Ann Hughes, Tessa Collingridge. Front row: Roger Edwards, Maxwell Poole, Peter Williams, Ronald Faulkner, Michael Parsons, Geoffrey Richards.

High Cross School class, 1955.

High Cross School class, June 1956. From left to right: Allan Fear, Robert Chopland, Margaret Tremayne, Robert Howells, Pamela Taylor, Susan Brock.

eight

Sport and Leisure

Soccer

Soccer arrived in Rogerstone in 1886 with the immigrant iron workers from Shropshire. The Rogerstone team were most certainly formed between 1886 and 1889 although no exact date is known. A second XI team was started in 1896 and believed to have played in the Newport & District League. The Rogerstone Rangers soccer side was formed sometime before the Second World War, playing on a field the other side of the railway behind The Nook and re-forming after the end of the war. Other teams included the High Cross Stars, Oaks United and Alcan AFC.

Cricket

In 1901 the Newport & District League was founded and Rogerstone were the inaugural winners of this league in that season and are still playing to this day. They were nicknamed the 'brown paper baggies' because they always turned up for matches carrying their kit in brown paper bags and were mainly immigrant workers from Shropshire who had arrived with Nettlefolds. They played on a field, now Wern Estate, until the mid-1920s. When Lord Tredegar gave the Welfare Grounds to the village, the Parish Council invited the cricket club to play there. They subsequently changed their name to the Rogerstone Welfare Cricket Club, a name they still use. Among presidents of the club were Lord Tredegar and Lord and Lady Forestier-Walker. The first cricket pavilion was a small wooden building with no facilities. Tydu House was used for teas and club meetings. In 1998 the club opened its new two-storey brick-built pavilion complete with all facilities. Alcan, Whiteheads and Rogerstone Power Station also had cricket teams along with the Newport Fugitives Club.

Golf

Ladyhill Golf Club was formed in Newport in 1903 but in 1911 moved to a superior site in Rogerstone at Great Oak Farm. The clubhouse, formerly named Derwen Fawr, which means Great Oak, is believed to have been built on the site of the great Golynos Oak. The Newport Golf Club at Great Oak was officially opened on 19 September 1912. Some of the players had remained at the Ladyhill course until 1922 when they were obliged to move due to a compulsory purchase order placed on the site, which was required for building purposes. The Tredegar Park Golf Club was officially opened on 31 May 1923 on the steep inclines of the Gaer Fort, moving onto the flat near Pye Corner in 1936. They remained on this site until 1999 when they relocated to a new clubhouse and course at Parc-y-Brain, Rogerstone.

Rogerstone Band

The idea for a band was conceived in the post-war celebratory period, but it was not until 1948, after several years of fund raising to purchase instruments, that the band was officially formed. The band progressed well in the late fifties and sixties to a good class 'B' band, their success building until in 1972 they were promoted to a class 'A' band. In 1975 they were invited to play in the European Championships in Belgium, one of only three UK bands there.

Rogerstone Association Football Team, season 1892/93. From left to right, back row: J. Williams, J. Davies, M. Picken, H. Wilde, G. Hampton, J. Picken, A. Colley, R. Fox. Middle row: R. Jones, J. Jones, J. Hayward (Captain), T. Lewis. Front row: F. Colley, J. Taylor, W. Evans. This is the oldest known photograph of the Rogerstone soccer team.

In 1893 Rogerstone were founder members of the South Wales and Monmouthshire League, their pitch being located between the old Nail Works and the River Ebbw. Some of the earliest recorded honours for Rogerstone AFC include:

Cup or League Winners 1892/93
South Wales and Monmouthshire Challenge Cup Winners 1896/97
South Wales League Winners 1897/98
South Wales League Champions 1900/01
Llanbradach Charity Cup Winners 1903/04
The Woodcock Cup Winners 1922/23
Newport & District First Division Champions 1922/23

Llanbradach Charity Cup Winners, 1903/04. From left to right, back row: R. Davies, J. Allender, W. Colley, J. Hayward, H.J. Williams (Trainer), E. Watkins, J. Millwaters, W. Dudley, H. Wylde. F. Owen, J. Evans. Middle row: J. Waites, M. Picken, T.R. Evans, J. Littlehales (Captain), C. Evans (Vice-Captain), J.H. Jones, T. Connors. Front row: S. Archer, J. Gooding, G. Jones, P.H. Colley, G. Cashmore.

Opposite, above: Rogerstone Football Club, *c.* 1947/48. Back row: T. Witcombe, L. Ray, G. Sheppard, A. Johnson, L. Driscoll, G. Redding, F. Jarman. Middle row: G. Clayton, J. Deakin, J. Dixon, B. Barton, E. Jones. Front row: S. Phillips, S. Morris.

Opposite, below: Rogerstone Football Club, *c.* 1953/54. From left to right, back row: T. Witcombe, J. Phelps, R. Fletcher, B. Walters, C. Bateman, G. Currier, G. Perrett, D. Hodson. Front row: L. Fletcher, B. Jones, B. Hodson, J. Jarrett, M. Allen.

Rogerstone Rangers AFC, *c.* 1954. From left to right, back row: Referee -?-, G. Clayton, B. Barnes, A. Johnson, V. Barnes, G. Sheppard, J. Deakin, W. Whitchard. Front row: J. Dixon, H. Phillips, F. Morgan, Seth Phillips, J. Phillips.

Opposite, above: Rogerstone Welfare Cricket Club, 1932. From left to right, back row: E. Bullock, W. Power, G. Dixon, C. Hayes, S. Walsh, R. Hyatt, B. Deakin, G. Hillman. Front row: E. Robinson, A. North, Lady Forestier-Walker, J. Davies, W. Williams. Sitting: R. Jones. Lord and Lady Forestier-Walker were presidents of the Cricket Club.

Opposite, below: Rogerstone Welfare Cricket Club, 1947. From left to right, back row: C. Price, E. Robinson, Mr Bentham, A. Jarrett, J. Davis, J. Sage. Middle row: H. Insley, L. Price, I. Brixey, J. Lewis, J. Stephens, -?-, H. Mathews, E. James, P. James, J. Beddow. Front row: D. Newall, F. Bentham, B. Thomas, L. Jones, T. Bentham.

Rogerstone Welfare Cricket Club, 1952. From left to right, back row: N. Beddow, H. Mathews, G. Tobitt, A. Johnson, F. Morgan, K. Lowery, I. Brixey, J. Bond, J. Lewis. Front row: J. Hunt, A. Joseph, F. Bentham, L. Price, E. Fawkes.

Derwen Fawr (Great Oak House), the home of Newport Golf Club.

In 1903 the Ladyhill Golf Club was formed securing the lease of the old Ladyhill Farmhouse and converting it into the first Clubhouse and Stewards quarters. Playing rights were established over Ladyhill Farm and parts of the adjoining Alway Farm. On 7 March 1903 the course formally opened with a match between W. Fernie, the Professional at Glamorgan Club, Penarth, and J. Chitty, the club's first Professional Greenkeeper. When the land at Ladyhill was required for housing, the Newport Golf Club moved to a superior site on farmland at Rogerstone. The move to Derwen Fawr took place in 1912 and the course was officially opened on 19 September 1912.

Derwen Fawr was part of the Golynos Estate, which had belonged to the Phillips family of Risca. The name Great Oak is believed to have been derived from the house being built on the site of the great Golynos Oak. A document held by the Newport Golf Club shows that Great Oak consisted of a small farm and outbuildings with some thirty-one and a half acres of land. The land was eventually purchased by the Golf Club in 1924 for the sum of £2,100 and purchasing of adjoining land followed over the years. During the war years, 1939-45, the clubhouse and course were open to all serving officers and the Americans stationed in the area took full advantage of the facilities, presenting a silver plaque to the club on leaving, in appreciation of the time they enjoyed there.

The clubhouse remains the same basic eighteenth- or nineteenth-century structure; the changes to meet members' needs keeping in mind the original house.

Opposite, below: Rogerstone Welfare Cricket Club 1965. From left to right, back row: S. Walsh, D. Williams, J. Edwards, G. Tobitt, D. Picken, M. Morgan, G. Lixton, A. Moise. Front row: B. O'Neill, B. Jones, J. Hackling, R. Phillips, J. Walsh.

The Rogerstone Welfare Air Rifle Club 19 June 1938. From left to right, back row: ? Hubbard, ? Rogers, W. Williams. Front row: Ted Green, Cliff Payne, Trevor Edwards (Captain), Glyn Ralph, Paddy O'Connor. The Rifle Club range was on the top floor of Tydu House, the target being in boxes on the wall at the far end of the room. They were the winners of the Newport & District Air Rifle League Champion Shield and Clarry Shield for the 1936/37 season. In 1937/38 they were winners of the League Cup and Royal Gwent Hospital Cup.

Opposite, above: The British Legion Ladies Skittle Team, 1946. From left to right, back row: Emily Littlehales, Veronica Bateman, Enid Hughes, Rose Haines. Front row: Murial Scott, Amy Dixon, Cissie Langley, Bertha Edwards.

Opposite, below: The British Legion Gold Badge presentation to Frank Perks by the Wales Area Organizer, with members from the branch and club standing behind them.

Rogerstone Band, pre-1914. Rogerstone had enjoyed a band in much earlier years as this photograph shows. Back row: second left: Joseph Aaron Picken, fifth left: Fred Bailey. Second row: second left: Tom Price, Mathias Rosser. The boy second from right is Bert Periam. Front row: Joseph A. Picken Jnr and right of drum William Lloyd.

Rogerstone Band 1950. The cup was for First Prize class D at Ferndale. From left to right, back row: Sid Holland, Fred Bailey, Bert Periam, John Symons, John Webster, Archie Everett, Bill Hoare, Ken Powles, Frank Jones, Billy Lloyd. Middle row: Alan Beale, Vernon Morgan, Tudor Jones, Charles Rees, Fred Morgan, Keith Mason, Edgar Bullock, John Phelps, Don Morgan, Cliff Goodwin, Barrie Williams, Les Williams, Tom Byrne, Ron Wilton. Boys: John Trew, John Holland, Keith Sully, Bob Sully. Front row: Eddie Found, Jim Morgan, Ron James, George Wilde, George Godden, Dr G.E. Hull (President), Grosvenor Hallett, W. 'Pop' Mamloff, Bill Morley.

A Band Social evening, *c.* 1950. An Entertainment Committee was formed in the early days of the band to organize events to raise money for replacement instruments, uniforms and so on. The committee consisted largely of friends and relations of band members. From 1948 to 1958 they organized the annual carnival and fête held at the Welfare Grounds. It was recorded on one occasion that over 8,000 people attended the fête. Many social evenings were arranged, usually held at St John's church hall or the British Legion Hall, and were usually very well attended.

Opposite, above: Rogerstone Band in 1950 leading the Whit Sunday March over the bridge from St John's Crescent onto Tregwilym Road. The bandmaster was George Godden.

Opposite, below: The band at Osnabruck Town Square 1966, taking part in British Week.

Monmouthshire County Youth Champions 1967. From left to right, back row: S. Thomas, A. Matthews, L. Archer, P. Roberts, W. Roberts, R. Powell, E. Taylor. Middle row: S. Mitchell, M. Needham, G. Pugh, C. Elliot, D. Osborne, ? Wright, G. Showell, ? Wright, D. Roberts. Front row: B. Axtell, S. Hough, V. Morgan, R. Rogers, Sam Roberts, N. Matthews, A. Thomas, P. Heal, B. Rogers.

In 1988 a forty year reunion was arranged and former members travelled from as far away as Manchester to attend. From left to right: Vernon Morgan, Don Morgan, Fred Morgan, John Webster, Ken Powles, John Symons, Les Williams, Keith Sully, Ron Wilton, Bob Sully, Ron James.

nine

Other Events

Officers of the 1st Company 2nd Volunteer Battalion South Wales Borderers, *c.* 1903. From left to right, top row: Sgt Fred Morgan, Sgt Tich Fenton, -?-, Sgt Tom Morgan. Front row: -?-, -?-, Capt. Jones, Col.-Sgt W. Dudley, -?-. Sergeant Fred Morgan was killed in France in 1915. Colour-Sergeant W. Dudley died in 1904, and details of his funeral were reported in the *South Wales Argus*.

Military Funeral at Rogerstone
Late Colour-Sergeant Dudley

South Wales Argus, Monday 14 November 1904

The remains of Colour-Sergeant W. Dudley, of the 1st Company 2nd Volunteer Battalion of the South Wales Borderers, Rogerstone, were interned at St John's churchyard on Saturday with full Military Honours. The deceased was well known throughout the district and had gained considerable popularity as being one of the most active members of the Volunteer Corps. This was shown by the large number who paid their last respects by forming one of the largest funerals ever known to have taken place in Rogerstone. Had he lived the present year out, Sergeant Dudley would have been the recipient of the long-service medal. However, he unfortunately contracted a cold, which brought on a severe attack of pneumonia, which had a fatal termination on Wednesday last. On Saturday the village of Rogerstone was in a state of mourning and the greatest sympathy was evidenced by the inhabitants towards his bereaved wife and family.

The procession lined up in the following order; Borderers being in command, Firing Party, Rogerstone Volunteers, in charge of Staff Sergeant, band of the 2nd V. B. South Wales Borderers, Newport (Bandmaster Dreyton), gun carriage containing the coffin and members of the Royal Field Artillery, Newport, Escort 2nd V.B. (I Company) South Wales Borderers, Rogerstone, ex-volunteers (ex-Sergeant J. Healey), Boys Brigade (Captain D Watkins), Major Badger, Sergeant Major English, Headquarters Company, Captain Frank Jones (late Captain of Rogerstone Corps), Staff-Sergeant, representing the 2nd V.B. Corps. South Wales Borderers of surrounding districts, members of the Hearts of Oak and Rogerstone Football Club, preceded by about 500 of the deceased's fellow workmen and friends. Wreaths were sent from the Staff Sergeants and Sergeants of the Borderers Sergeants' mess, Sergeant instructor and Sergeants 2nd V.B. (I Company) South Wales Borderers, Rogerstone, Sergeants mess 4th V. B. South Wales Borderers, Boys Brigade, Football Club (Rogerstone), Guest, Keen & Nettlefold Ltd., workmen, and Mr John Williams (Manager). In addition there were a large number sent from the relatives and friends of the deceased. The burial service was conducted by the curate, the Rev. W. S. Stubbs, and six Colour Sergeants of the 2nd V. B. South Wales Borderers acted as bearers. At the conclusion of the service at the graveside the 'Last Post' was sounded by the 2nd V.B. Bugle Band.

The funeral of Charles and Mary Thomas held at Bethesda Chapel, Rogerstone. In the criminal history of Monmouthshire few cases have aroused more interest, or inspired a greater feeling of horror than that in connection with which William Butler has been called upon to pay the extreme penalty of the law. *South Wales Argus*, 24 March 1910. The brutal murder of an elderly couple Charles and Mary Thomas of Tank Cottage, Bassaleg, took place on the night of 11 November 1909. The couple were battered to death in their beds. On 15 November, William Butler, (real name William Clements of Gloucester), was arrested and charged with the double murder. After a two-day trial at Monmouth in February 1910, he was found guilty and taken to Usk Prison where he was executed on 24 March 1910.

The funeral of the murdered couple took place at Bethesda Chapel of which Mr and Mrs Thomas were much loved and respected members. Hundreds lined the route from Bassaleg to Bethesda and all blinds along the way were drawn. The chapel was unable to accommodate the great number of people who wished to attend the funeral.

Rogerstone fire brigade, pre-1914. Back row: third from left is Steve Furlong, second from right is Fred Morgan. Front row: second from left is Harry Cornish. This photograph was taken at the rear of Tydu Infants' School.

Minutes of the fire brigade committee at Rogerstone fire station dated 20 July 1911 until 3 April 1914 mostly contain notes on the upkeep of the fire station buildings and grounds, uniforms and suggested appointees for vacancies as they arose. The fire engine was a handcart on two wheels that was pulled along by the firemen. They could often be seen practising pulling the cart along Tregwilym Road, Cefn Road and High Cross Road and Lane. In correspondence dated June 1914 a request was made for uniforms for two officers and ten men. A fireman would often have to tender his resignation if his employment took him out of the Rogerstone district. The fire station building was situated on Tregwilym Road, near to the present-day entrance to Alcan.

Above: Election Campaign 1926/27, canvassing at James Street, Rogerstone. Eliza Evans is shaking hands with Sir Leolin Forestier-Walker. From left to right: Alf Turbeville (chauffeur to Sir Leolin), Maud Bentham (*née* Price of No. 10 James Street), Bernard Davies, Eliza Evans (of No. 13 James Street), Alec Colley, Bill Bullock, Lady Forestier-Walker, Sir Leolin Forestier-Walker, Jack Parker (who was at the relief of Ladysmith, South Africa and became known locally as 'Ladysmith'), Margaret Parker, daughter of Jack (of No. 8 James Street), Joe Littlehales (previously a professional footballer with Aston Villa), Edgar Brown (Secretary at GKN who eventually became a Managing Director), Olive Davies, Gladys Dudley (of No. 14 James Street).

Above, left: Private Jim Irving, served in the UK and Middle East as a cook during the First World War. He was born in Risca but lived in Rogerstone from 1925 until his death in 1949.

Above, right: Trevor Edwards, signal sergeant, Home Guards, 1939-45.

Right: Alfred Picken, Dunkirk Veteran, at Antwerp, April 1945. He was in service throughout the war.

ARP, 1940.

Children in a field near the Myrtle Grove, where the army set up camp in 1941. From left to right, standing: Geoffrey Willis, Sidney Vaughn, Fred Butler, Vivian Davies, (baby) Edwin Phillips, Seth Phillips, Grovenor Phillips (at back). Kneeling: Mary Butler, Delphine Lovell. Sitting: Betty Willis, Jean Willis, Rose Willis.

Children's street party at McLean Street to celebrate the coronation in 1953.

In 1953 the Rogerstone Parish Council issued this notice:

Coronation Celebrations

In connection with Rogerstone Coronation Celebrations ALL HOUSEHOLDERS are urged to DECORATE their houses in the gay atmosphere of the coronation. The Parish Council are pleased to offer 3 prizes (1st, 2nd & 3rd) for the best decorated dwelling houses, and are confident of your wholehearted co-operation in making this aspect of the celebrations a marked success. The houses will be judged by a Panel of Judges on the evening of 1st June, and the results announced on Coronation Day, at the Welfare Grounds.

Luncheon was also provided for the Old Age Pensioners of the parish and the celebrations at the Welfare Grounds included sideshow and sporting events for young and old alike.

Above and below: Coronation Party, Ifor Hael Road, 1953.

A photograph of Moira James and Leighton Wilde, *c.* 1946. They won a prize of 5s (2nd prize?). Leighton's suit was made by Mrs James out of her old blackout curtains and his top hat was made by Mr Wilde out of stiff cardboard and painted a shiny black. Mr Wilde also grew the sweet-peas used in Moira's bouquet. Moira's dress, headdress and veil were lent to her by a colleague of her aunt's – they were her confirmation dress and veil. The photograph was taken at Moira's home in the Uplands before they left for the Carnival.

Carnival time at The Nook, *c.* 1939.

The Ida Teachum Formation Team – winners of the first prize at Rogerstone Carnival 1951. Left to right: Margaret Stephens (West Works Canteen), Kitty Thomas (Cafeteria Supervisor), Ethel Morgan (Canteen Supervisor).

The Alcan Canteen Ladies at the Carnival, 1959. Left to right: E. Morgan, A. Faulkner, A. Stanworth, M. Johnson, M. Stephens, K. Thomas. Seated: Ann ?.

Street Party at Charles Street, *c.* 1950.

Carnival bride and groom. The groom is Nancy Oliver and the bride Peggy Robinson. Nancy won First Prize. Also in the photograph are Don Robberts, Gwen Purnell, Nobby Taylor and Gwyneth Clayton.

Carnival Float on Cefn Road, *c.* 1963. Third left is Nancy Howells and extreme right is Jean Harbon.

Right: Rogerstone Power Station Fête, 1965. PC Roger Morgan, age five, is making the arrest.

Opposite, below: Rogerstone Carnival, 1969.

Below: Carnival Float High Cross Estate, *c.* 1967.

Carnival Floats making their way up Tregwilym Road towards the Welfare Grounds, c. 1966. Stan Lewis' wireless and electrical shop can be seen at the front of the house on the right. This photograph shows the houses opposite the library before they were demolished.

In this photograph John's Farm is visible on the left.

Alcan Singers, 1982. Their debut performance at the Alcan Club. The conductor was Mr Marsden Walsh and Mr Ray Norris was on piano. The members included: Bill Harris, Malcolm Pritchard, Brian Jones, John Mayberry, Les Reed, Mervyn Jones, Philip Gittings, Peter Faulkner, Bob James, Bronco Griffiths, Bill Alan, Eddie Lee, Ken Hopkins, Cecil Wilcox, Cecil Phillips, Basil Jones, Stan Williams, Cyril Thomas and Len Carter.

Alcan Pantomime, 1948. Pantomimes were a popular feature of the social life of the works.

Other local titles published by Tempus

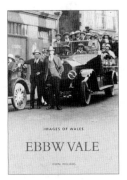

Ebbw Vale
IDWAL WILLIAMS

Ebbw Vale's strong industrial history is well represented in this comprehensive collection of nearly 200 archive images, some of which date from as early as the 1900s. This book recalls life as it once was before the huge loss of steel industry jobs, and depicts the history of this part of Gwent in terms of its society, its culture and its industry. With pictures as varied as Rassau Road street scenes and miners's strikes, this book is a fast-moving glimpse of this area's bustling history.
0 7524 3209 5

Newport East of the River
RACHAEL ANDERTON

This long-awaited companion to Newport, West of the River, provides a fascinating pictorial journey around the east side of the River Usk in Newport, South Wales. Compiled using over 200 photographs from the Newport Museum and Art Gallery, this is a vibrant history of the changes that have taken place over the last 150 years.
0 7524 2462 9

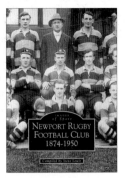

Newport Rugby Football Club 1874-1950
STEVE LEWIS

This book contains a vast collection of images and accompanying text which illustrate the first 76 years Newport Rugby Club. From its formation 1874 the club's history is full of great achievements and great names from the game of Rugby Union, as depicted here through a fascinating mixture of action shots, player portraits and printed memorabilia.
0 7524 1570 0

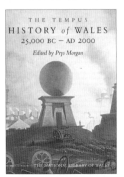

The Tempus History of Wales
PRYS MORGAN

Wales was at the heart of the Industrial Revolution, towns like Merthyr Tydfil driving the engine of the British Empire. The cultural and social divide between modern, industrialised Wales and the traditional agricultural areas is explored within this comprehensive volume.
0 7524 1983 8

If you are interested in purchasing other books published by Tempus, or in case you have difficulty finding any Tempus books in your local bookshop, you can also place orders directly through our website

www.tempus-publishing.com